HEARING ALL SIDES
Resolving Conflicts

About the Series Authors

Jeanette Phillips is principal of the Tenaya Middle School in Fresno, California. She has been a middle-school principal for the past 19 years and before that served as a vice-principal and as a teacher in grades K-12. Jeanette was a co-founder of the California League of Middle Schools in 1978 and continues to serve on its board as Program Chair. She was a member of the Executive Council and Board of Directors for the National Middle School Association for six years and served as the association's President in 1990–91. She received the Distinguished Service Award from the National Middle School Association in 1992, the ACSA Outstanding Educator Award and the California League of Middle Schools President's Award in 1992.

Carl Zon has been a teacher, counselor, and administrator in elementary, middle, and high schools in the states of Illinois, Wisconsin, and California. He is currently on the staff of the California League of Middle Schools and California League of High Schools. As a consultant, he has assisted schools and districts with interdisciplinary unit design and made presentations on interdisciplinary instruction as state and national conferences. He has also been a contributing author on many CLMS monographs. He is past president of the California League of Middle Schools and a recipient of the CLMS President's Award for Exceptional Service to Middle Level Education in California (1992).

Adapted from a Unit by these Teachers

Bill Jones has taught earth science and music at Day Middle School in Newton, MA, for seventeen years. He is an active musician, and directs student musicals and cabaret performances. He has consulted on "Transformations," a science series for middle school students and has composed the music for a PBS series dealing with drugs and alcohol and young children.

Marj Montgomery is an eighth-grade teacher of American history and English at Day Middle School in Newton, MA. She has developed her eighth graders as teacher trainers, and wherever possible, turns session over to them. Marj and Bill have been working together on an eighth-grade team for ten years. They have developed interdisciplinary curricula on whales and whaling, westering, the river, and evolution/creationism.

Mary Morganti is an eighth-grade teacher and math department chair at Bigelow Middle School in Newton, MA. In addition to teaching algebra and pre-algebra, she teaches a course that explores the connections between and among math, art, architecture, and nature. She is a long-time math team coach. Over the past eleven years, she has been recognized for various community service programs she has initiated with her students.

Acknowledgments

Cover Design: Suzanne Schineller
Cover Photo: Rick Iwasaki/Tony Stone Images

Printed in the United States of America.
ISBN: 0-13-412503-7
    6 7 8 9 10   02 01 00

TABLE OF CONTENTS

ABOUT INTERDISCIPLINARY UNITS

Successful instructional practices make strong connections between the structure and substance of subject area disciplines and the developmental characteristics of young adolescents. Interdisciplinary learning experiences are particularly appropriate for demonstrating not only the complexity, richness, and "connectedness" of knowledge but also its usefulness and application in the lives of students. Well-planned interdisciplinary units show the world operating as a whole, lend coherence to concepts otherwise isolated within specific disciplines, and empower students to use disciplines in concert and to compare and contrast them.

Hearing All Sides: Resolving Conflict is an interdisciplinary unit that brings together discipline-based and interdisciplinary perspectives. The unit has been designed using a step-by-step model adapted by Carl Zon and Laurie Aboudara-Robertson from the work of H. H. Jacobs (1989) and Jacobs and J. H. Borland (1986). These steps are described below.

Selecting and Defining an Organizing Center

Unit development begins with the selection of a topic or organizing center such as a theme, subject area(s), event, issue or problem. The topic needs to generate interdisciplinary exploration and be interesting and relevant to students. James Beane (1993) has defined eleven themes that express the intersection of young adolescent concerns and more global social concerns. The theme of "transitions" intersects with these categories of concerns—*understanding personal changes and living in a changing world*. Concepts and generalizations in state and national curriculum frameworks can also assist in unifying disciplines. Current events, including those in students' daily lives, can be particularly engaging for young learners.

Once a topic is chosen, teachers should explore it by using a spoked wheel as a graphic organizer. The wheel, or organizing center, includes a hub for the topic and spokes for each discipline. Teachers use brainstorming (Osborne, 1963) to define discipline-based perspectives on the chosen topic. Brainstormed associations, including concepts, generalizations, materials, and people, are written next to the related disciplinary spoke(s).

Creating a Scope-and-Sequence of Guiding Questions

The next step entails organizing the brainstormed associations and creating a scope-and-sequence of guiding questions for the unit. Brainstorming can once again be used to formulate a tentative list of questions. Students can be involved in this process.

Each guiding question should be general in nature, somewhat like a chapter heading in a textbook. The set of questions, three to six in number, must transcend disciplinary lines, flow in a logical sequence, be sensitive to time constraints, lead to answers students need to know, and be stated in language students comprehend. Study of each question should occupy about one week.

Developing Master and Individual Activity Plans

The guiding questions are now used to develop master and individual activity plans that engage students in purposeful inquiry. Bloom's Taxonomy (1956) provides a model of cognition that can guide the design of an array of activities that elicit critical and creative thinking including: knowledge acquisition, comprehension, application, analysis, synthesis, and evaluation. Master activity plans, prepared as an overview for each guiding question, summarize individual activities and list required resources.

Individual activity plans for each guiding question contain: the overall activity plan or objective; possible student groupings for the activity; Bloom's thinking process(es) highlighted in the activity; procedures for carrying out the activity; products and outcomes; standards (quality, quantity, and time); resources needed; and an evaluation scheme.

Designing an Evaluation Scheme

A comprehensive evaluation scheme is at the heart of successful interdisciplinary teaching and learning. Given the effort required to develop these experiences and the significant departure from traditional discipline-based instruction they represent, teachers must define standards meticulously and capture evidence of student growth assiduously.

Engaging activities including projects are necessary but insufficient guarantees that students benefit from interdisciplinary experiences. Effective evaluation strategies start with thoughtfully selected organizing centers, carefully stated guiding questions, and clearly defined standards and performance expectations for each activity. Students can keep journals and portfolios to document their responses to guiding questions. They can also participate in defining evaluation criteria for their products and performances.

Finally, teachers must define the value-added dimension of interdisciplinary learning by answering this critical question: "What knowledge, skills and habits of mind do we value in students as interdisciplinary learners?"Otherwise stated, teachers must design interdisciplinary experiences that provide evidence to answer these questions: What is it about interdisciplinary learning that students cannot acquire without using this approach? Are inter

disciplinary learners more likely to see connections between disciplines spontaneously? Do they draw cross-disciplinary insights more frequently? Do they use their knowledge from one discipline to strengthen their understanding of the concepts in another? Are they better synthesizers or holistic thinkers?

Heidi Hayes Jacobs has stated: "With its promise of unifying knowledge and modes of understanding, interdisciplinary education represents the pinnacle of curriculum development" (Jacobs, 1989). You are invited to the "pinnacle" of curriculum design and offered this model to assist you in meeting the interdisciplinary learning needs of young adolescents.

—Carl Zon

BIBLIOGRAPHY

Beane, J. A. (1993): A middle school curriculum: From rhetoric to reality; Columbus, OH, National Middle School Association.

Bloom, B.S., ed. (1956): Taxonomy of educational objectives: The classification of educational goals, handbook 1: Cognitive domain; New York, NY, David Mckay.

Cohen, M. (November 1978): "Whatever happened to interdisciplinary education?" Educational Leadership.

Jacobs, H. H. (1989): Interdisciplinary curriculum: Design and implementation; Alexandria, VA; Association for Supervision and Curriculum Development.

Jacobs, H. H., & Borland, J. H. (Winter 1986): "The interdisciplinary concept model: Design and implementation," Gifted Child Quarterly.

Osborn, A. F. (1963): Applied imagination; New York, NY; Charles Scribner and Company.

Owen, M. (1996): Skills for Resolving Conflict (six-book series); Upper Saddle River, NJ; Globe Fearon.

ABOUT THIS UNIT

Differences of opinion are inevitable. But it is when differences of opinion are not heard, let alone respected, that disagreement boils over into conflict. The purpose of *Hearing All Sides: Resolving Conflict* is to help students learn to truly hear what others are saying, to state what they themselves want clearly and in non-threatening ways when faced with problems, to respect the views of others, and to find ways to negotiate solutions so that no one loses.

Note that some activities in this unit deal with what causes anger and how anger is expressed. Such activities may be upsetting to some students and you should monitor student reactions closely. If you feel an activity may be too upsetting, you may choose to eliminate it.

The activities in the first Guiding Question help students to see how stressful conflict can be, why conflicts arise, and why using conflict resolution strategies can be valuable. They see that reasons for national and global conflicts are similar to those for conflicts between individuals.

Guiding Question 2 deals with strategies for keeping disagreements from boiling over into conflict, a metaphor used in the first lesson in the section. Subsequent lessons have students using readings, role plays, and activities to explore noncombative word choices, tone of voice, and body language. Students also try out good listening skills to keep conversations from coming to impasse. They also learn techniques to "calm down" when they begin to lose their temper in disagreements.

The final Guiding Question involves students in developing strategies for coming to win-win solutions and then asks them to practice these strategies. Students not only see how fictional characters resolve their problems in role plays, they also observe how they solve disagreements with other students while working on unit activities.

The time frame for each lesson is based on a regular class period. However, Homeroom, Advisory, and Guidance also present excellent opportunities for using this unit. Activities may be adapted, shortened, or omitted to fit these shorter time frames. For example, to shorten Activity 1.1, the mock test might be omitted, and to shorten 2.6, students might complete the activity working as individuals rather than in groups.

INTERDISCIPLINARY WHEEL

MATH

* taking blood pressure

LANGUAGE ARTS

* journal writing
* rewriting a story
* writing poems
* oral presentations
* analyzing a poem, a reading
* publishing
* practicing listening skills

ORGANIZING CENTER

Resolving Conflict

SCIENCE

* taking blood pressure

SOCIAL STUDIES

* analyzing global conflict
* categorizing stressors
* role playing
* creating a continuum
* negotiating
* determining point of view

HEALTH/PHYSICAL EDUCATION

* taking blood pressure
* recognizing anger triggers
* practicing appropriate body language
* distinguishing tone of voice
* practicing listening skills
* practicing relaxation exercises

THE ARTS

* illustrating stress levels
* acting conflict and conflict resolution scenarios
* illustrating relaxation ideas

Source: Adapted from the work of Heidi Hayes Jacobs, 1988, by Carl Zon, Laurie Aboudara-Robertson, and the California League of Middle Schools.

Organizing Theme: Resolving Conflict

Guiding questions:

1. What is conflict?

2. What are some skills that will help me prevent/resolve conflict?

3. How can negotiating lead to win-win solutions?

Source: Adapted from the work of Heidi Hayes Jacobs, 1988, by Carl Zon, Laurie Aboudara-Robertson and the Redwood Middle School, and the California League of Middle Schools.

GUIDING QUESTION 1: What is conflict?

Activities/Description	Math	Science	Language Arts	Social Studies	Health	The Arts	Time
1.1 Recognizing the Effects of Stress Related to Conflict—monitoring heart rate and blood pressure before and after a stressful situation	✔	✔	✔	✔	✔	✔	1 class period
1.2 Analyzing the Causes of Conflict—categorizing causes of conflict, defining the elements present in any conflict			✔	✔			1 class period
1.3 Recognizing the Value of Conflict Resolution Strategies—analyzing the pros and cons of learning conflict resolution strategies			✔	✔	✔		1 class period

1.1 RECOGNIZING THE EFFECTS OF STRESS RELATED TO CONFLICT

GUIDING QUESTION 1:   What is conflict?

SUBJECT AREAS: All

GROUPING: Whole class, pairs

MATERIALS: Electronic blood pressure machine

BLOOM'S TAXONOMY LEVEL: Knowledge, Comprehension, Analysis

PRODUCTS AND OUTCOMES: List of stressful people or situations

TIME FRAME: 1 class period

Procedure:

Pre-class preparation: If you are not in a teaming situation, to introduce the topic of conflict resolution to your students, work with the science or health teacher or school nurse to prepare a brief lesson on heart rate and blood pressure. As the two of you begin the lesson, explain that this information is now a required part of the school curriculum and you have agreed to use part of your class time to have it taught.

1. Ask students to suggest their definitions of blood pressure (the pressure exerted by the blood against the inner walls of the blood vessels, such as the arteries and the heart).

   Draw a diagram of the heart on the chalkboard and write *diastolic pressure* and *systolic pressure*. Explain each while showing the action of the heart on the diagram (diastolic: rhythmic dilation of the heart, especially the ventricles, following each contraction during which the heart relaxes and the chambers fill with blood; systolic: the rhythmic contraction of the heart, especially the ventricles, during which the blood is driven onward from the chambers).

   Explain what is considered the normal range of blood pressure for different ages, what blood pressure indicates about one's health, how high blood pressure is an indication of medical problems, and how blood pressure can be controlled by weight, exercise, and decreasing stress. Emphasize that blood pressure as well as heart rate both increase when one's emotions are aroused.

2. Ask for a volunteer and, using the electronic blood pressure machine, take the student's blood pressure, showing the class how the machine is used. Explain what the two numbers in the reading mean.

   Have the student take his or her own pulse to determine heart beats per minute.

3. Draw a table on the board and title the columns: Heart Rate, Blood Pressure. Then divide the class into pairs. Have student pairs take each other's pulse rates and blood pressures. When all pairs are done, have each read the data it obtained aloud while you or a class recorder lists the information on the board. Determine the average heart rate and blood pressure for the class as a whole.

4. Look at your watch and tell your teacher colleague that you are sorry, but you need to stop the heart rate/blood pressure lesson and give the students a surprise quiz. Use some plausible reason, such as the students, not having had enough quizzes for the marking period.

Distribute a brief quiz or dictate a brief quiz based on work students are currently doing in your class. Make the questions ambiguous or a little more advanced than usual for your quizzes. While the students are working, interrupt with a constant stream of distractions: noise; reminders to students that some other assignment is due and when; directions, some contradictory; comments such as "This is a timed test," "This is important for your final grade," "One wrong is a C; two wrong is an F."

When students begin to show their distress at the test and the interruptions, stop the activity and explain that you wanted to simulate conditions of stress so that students could see what stress does to their blood pressure and heart rate.

5. Have students break into pairs again and take their heart rates and blood pressures. Have a recorder again list the data on the board and have the class determine the new averages.

6. Discuss with the class how stress can affect health—even the health of young people. Ask the class as a whole to list physical reactions to stress (sweaty palms, butterflies, muscle tension, increased heart rate, red face, and so on).

Alternative: If you are using this unit in an advisory, homeroom, or guidance setting, omit steps 4 and 5 and begin with step 6.

Assignment: Have students think about the situations or people that cause them stress and list three such situations or people for the next class. Be sure to indicate that any extremely personal concerns be saved for discussion with you rather than in class.

Evaluation:

Students should be able to explain what a blood pressure reading shows.

Students should be able to describe the relationship between stress and increased heart rate and blood pressure.

1.2 ANALYZING THE CAUSES OF CONFLICT

GUIDING QUESTION 1:   What is conflict?

SUBJECT AREAS: Social Studies, Language Arts

GROUPING: Whole class, small groups, pairs

MATERIALS: Understanding the Roots of Conflict activity sheet

BLOOM'S TAXONOMY LEVEL: Knowledge, Comprehension, Analysis, Synthesis

PRODUCTS AND OUTCOMES: Completed Understanding the Roots of Conflict activity sheets, journal entries

TIME FRAME: 1 class period

Procedure:

1. Have three or four volunteers read aloud their lists of people and/or situations that cause stress from Activity 1.1. Record their answers on the board. To end this step, ask for any other items not already listed and write them on the board.

2. Divide the class into small groups and have each group categorize the list of personal stressors. Categories might include some of the following: problems with parents, problems with friends, boyfriend/girlfriend problems, fights, harassment or hassling, rumors, communication problems, money problems, and so on.

3. After 7 to 10 minutes, reassemble the class and ask for recorders to read their group's categories. List the categories on the board and discuss each one until students have reached consensus on what the categories should be. Point out that conflict is the underlying theme in many of the situations and relationships listed, and that stress is often a result, or effect, of conflict.

   Draw a vertical line next to the list of personal stressors and ask students to list national/global sources of conflict. As a class, categorize these situations. Possible categories might be racism, economic problems, territorial disputes, and so on.

4. Ask students to define *conflict*. Their definition should have the following elements: (1.) two or more groups or individuals, (2.) the belief or viewpoint that each one's wants (resources, needs) are (3.) incompatible with the other's wants (resources, needs).

5. Have students in pairs test out the class's definition by completing the Understanding the Roots of Conflict activity sheet. Then reconvene the class and discuss students' sheets until a consensus can be reached on a definition incorporating the three elements listed in Step 4. Emphasize in your discussion that national and global situations, like individuals' conflicts, have the same three elements.

6. Explain to students that disagreements are inevitable because people and nations don't think alike or want the same things, but that honest disagreements are typically not confrontational.

Assignment: Ask students to write journal entries describing how an honest disagreement between two people might escalate into a conflict.

For extra credit have one or two volunteers create a poster(s) with the class's definition of conflict for display while students are working on this unit.

Evaluation:
Students should be able to define *conflict*.

Students should be able to distinguish between honest disagreements and conflicts.

Students should be able to identify several causes of conflict—on a personal level and on the national/global level.

UNDERSTANDING THE ROOTS OF CONFLICT

1. Choose one individual source of conflict and answer the following questions. Source of conflict:

   _____

   a. Who are the individuals or groups involved?

   _____

   b. What is the competing belief or viewpoint?

   _____

   _____

   c. What is the competing resource or need of each individual or group?

   _____

   _____

   _____

   _____

2. Choose one national or global source of conflict and answer the following questions. Source of conflict:

   _____

   a. Who are the individuals or groups involved?

   _____

   b. What is the competing belief or viewpoint?

   _____

   _____

   c. What is the competing resource or need of each individual or group?

   _____

   _____

   _____

   _____

1.3 RECOGNIZING THE VALUE OF CONFLICT RESOLUTION STRATEGIES

GUIDING QUESTION 1:   What is conflict?

SUBJECT AREAS: Social Studies, Health, Language Arts

GROUPING: Whole class, small groups, pairs

MATERIALS: Conflict Management activity sheet

BLOOM'S TAXONOMY LEVEL: Knowledge, Comprehension, Analysis, Evaluation

PRODUCTS AND OUTCOMES: Completed Conflict Management activity sheets, journal entries

TIME FRAME: 1 class period

Procedure:

1. Ask several volunteers to describe how an honest difference of opinion can escalate into a conflict with name calling, yelling at each other, door slamming, the involvement of third parties on one side or the other, and so on. If students recount actual situations, they should be encouraged to disguise them by using made-up names. As students describe situations, list on the board each step that escalated the disagreement. Possibilities include: one person talking while the other was talking, introduction of extraneous information to cloud the central issue, or the use of ridicule or sarcasm.

2. Ask students how they feel after they argue with friends or relatives. Tell them that learning conflict resolution strategies can help them learn to solve disagreements before they escalate into conflict.

3. Divide the class into groups and distribute the Conflict Management activity sheet. After 10 minutes, reassemble the class and lead a discussion on the benefits of learning and using conflict resolution strategies.

4. Point out that learning how to manage conflict will improve students' listening, problem-solving, and decision-making skills. Ask students to speculate in their journals about why this might be true.

Evaluation:

Students should be able to describe the value of using conflict resolution strategies in handling disagreements.

CONFLICT MANAGEMENT

1. The table below lists some of the consequences of conflict. For each consequence, write a benefit of learning how to resolve conflicts. Add any other consequences and benefits that you can think of.

Consequences of conflict	Benefits of resolving conflict
Hostility	Decreases hostility
Violence	
Poor self-esteem	
Divides friends/families	
Stress	
Uses up time	
Uses up emotional energy	
Other	

2. a. Think of a national or global conflict.

_____

b. On a seperate sheet of paper (or the back of this one), explain which, if any, of the benefits above apply to a resolution of that conflict.

MASTER ACTIVITY PLAN

GUIDING QUESTION: What are some skills that will help me prevent/resolve conflict?

Activities/Description	Math	Science	Language Arts	Social Studies	Health	The Arts	Time
2.1 Recognizing Anger Triggers—determining words and phrases that trigger anger, making a graphic representation of anger triggers			✔	✔	✔	✔	1 class period
2.2 Analyzing the Importance of What You Say—using basic guidelines to good communication to analyze a reading about conflict, rewriting the story			✔	✔	✔		3 class periods
2.3 Recognizing the Importance of How You Say It—distinguishing between appropriate and inappropriate tone of voice for conflict resolution, role playing a conflict situation altering tone of voice			✔	✔	✔		1 class period
2.4 Understanding How Body Language Can Contribute to Conflict—differentiating between positive and negative body language, practicing positive body language			✔	✔	✔		1 class period
2.5 Determining Active Listening Skills—analyzing active listening, identifying and practicing active listening skills			✔	✔	✔	✔	1-2 class periods
2.6 Learning Ways to "Calm Down"—identifying techniques to control one's anger/emotions, creating a representation of these techniques				✔	✔	✔	1 or 2 class periods

2.1 RECOGNIZING ANGER TRIGGERS

GUIDING QUESTION 2: What are some skills that will help me prevent/resolve conflicts?

SUBJECT AREAS: Social Studies, Health, Language Arts, the Arts

GROUPING: Whole class, small groups, individuals

MATERIALS: Anger Triggers activity sheets, 1 per student

BLOOM'S TAXONOMY LEVEL: Comprehension, Analysis, Application, Evaluation

PRODUCTS AND OUTCOMES: Completed Anger Triggers activity sheets, journal entries/graphic representations about anger triggers

TIME FRAME: 1 class period

CAUTION: This activity may be upsetting to some students. Depending on the climate in your school and the maturity of your students, you may wish to set limits on this lesson, delete it, or closely monitor student reactions.

Procedure:

1. Introduce students to the metaphor of the boiling point. At a certain point, increased heat under a pan of water will cause the water to boil; as one's anger increases, the person will ultimately lose his/her temper. Point out that the effect of some words and actions on a person's anger can be just like turning up the heat under a pot of water on the stove. Those words or actions can be called "anger triggers."

2. Divide the class into groups and ask them to brainstorm answers to the question: What are some of the words and actions that make people angry? Some examples are:
   • "Who cares? It's no big deal."
   • "You're so stupid. No wonder you don't have any friends."
   • "I'm never going to trust you with anything of mine again."
   • "Bug off. I'm busy."
   • Walking away in the middle of an argument
   • Slamming the door
   • Taking my boom box

3. After about 5 minutes, moving quickly around the room, have each group add an item to the list that makes people angry or more angry.

Have a recorder write each one on the board. Be sure the list contains at least eight actions or words/word groups.

4. With students still in groups, distribute the Anger Triggers activity sheets, one per student. Return to the metaphor of boiling water again and introduce the markings on the stove dial as similar to the levels of a person's temper. As the stove dial is turned up, the heat under a pan of water increases, making it boil more rapidly. So, too, some words and actions will increase a person's anger and cause him/her to lose his/her temper.

Ask students to decide as groups where each item from the list on the board belongs on the stove dial on the activity sheets. Would a situation, action, or set of words cause mild anger or annoyance? Or would it cause a person to reach the boiling point?

There will be disagreements about where each item should be placed. When a number of disagreements arise, stop the groups' discussions and have the students determine what is causing the disagreements. They should come to realize that whether something is an anger trigger for any one person depends on who says the words or does the action, and the history of the speaker's or actor's relationship to the person. They should also recognize that their own history governs the degree of anger they feel over any situation or action.

Assignment: Have students draw in their journals stove dials showing two or three situations or actions that would trigger anger in them and explain why. How would they change the situation or action so that they would not be so bothered?

Evaluation:
Students should show an awareness of anger triggers—their own and others.

Students should be able to explain that an anger trigger for one person may not be the same as an anger trigger for another person and that each person because of his/her experience has idiosyncratic anger triggers.

ANGER TRIGGERS

What makes people angry? How angry can they get? List anger triggers around the stove dial where you think they belong.

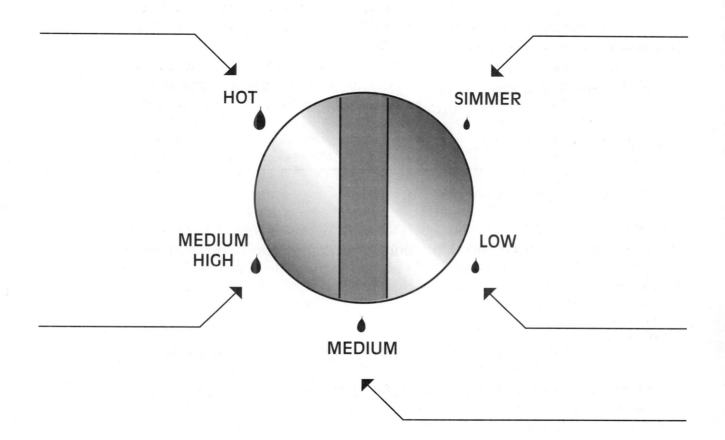

HOT

SIMMER

MEDIUM
HIGH

LOW

MEDIUM

2.2 ANALYZING THE IMPORTANCE OF WHAT YOU SAY

GUIDING QUESTION 2: What are some skills that will help me prevent/resolve conflicts?

SUBJECT AREAS: Social Studies, Language Arts, Health

GROUPING: Whole class, pairs

MATERIALS: Let's Fight reading sheets, 1 per student
Let's Solve the Problem reading sheets, 1 per student
Saying It Another Way activity sheets, 1 per student

BLOOM'S TAXONOMY LEVEL: Knowledge, Comprehension, Analysis, Synthesis, Application, Evaluation

PRODUCTS AND OUTCOMES: Revised versions of the Let's Fight story, journal entries, completed Saying It Another Way activity sheets

TIME FRAME: 3 class periods

Procedure:

Period 1

1. "Sticks and stones can break my bones, but names can never hurt me." Ask students if they think this old saying is true. After a brief discussion as warm up, point out that name-calling is one of the ways a disagreement can escalate into a conflict.

   Distribute the Let's Fight sheets and have students read their copies.

   After students have read the story once, ask them to reread it and underline each statement or action that escalated the conflict.

2. Write the following guidelines for good communication on the board:

   • Identify the problem and focus on the solution.

   • Don't blame: Use *I* rather than *You*.

   • Don't use absolutes like *never* and *always*.

   • Don"t name call.

   As a class discussion, go through the story and see how Sonya violated each guideline of good communication.

   • *Identify the problem and focus on the solution:* Sonya wanted Jamal to apologize and to promise to do better in the future; instead she focused on telling him how angry she was and how bad he was. Sometimes in the heat of anger and hurt feelings, it is difficult to keep from blaming the other person, but if the goal is to identify the problem (forgetting work time) and to try to see that the situation does not occur again (Jamal remembers), then the focus of the conversation should be on change and not on blaming.

- *Don't blame: Use* I *rather than* You: Sonya spent much of the time telling Jamal what she thought of him rather than how she felt. By focusing on how you feel, you avoid making the other person feel that he/she is being blamed or attacked and increase the likelihood that your concerns will be heard. Often when people feel blamed, they stop listening.
- *Don't use absolutes like* never *and* always: Using words like *sometimes* and *often* will keep the conversation from getting sidetracked into arguments over numbers.
- *Don't name call:* Jamal called himself stupid, trying to ease the problem and Sonya jumped right in and added to the name calling.

What other things did Sonya and Jamal do to turn the problem into a conflict? (Sonya started the conversation in anger; walked out on the argument)

Assignment: Ask students to list in their journals ways that Sonya could have handled the problem with Jamal more effectively.

Period 2

1. Divide the class into pairs and have each pair rewrite the Let's Fight story so that Sonya is able to tell Jamal how she feels without getting angry or making Jamal angry. Remind them to use the guidelines of good communication.

2. Have several pairs read aloud their revised stories and have the class critique them to see how well Sonya and Jamal solved their problem. Student pairs may choose to act out their versions of the story.

3. Distribute the Let's Solve the Problem reading for students to compare their versions. Have them rework any part of their stories that they think should be improved.

Assignment: If students are going to watch any TV shows, have them list violations of the guidelines for good communication they observe and then describe what the characters should have done instead.

Period 3

Follow-up: Have students share their observations from television viewing as a warm-up for the third day's discussion of word choice and its place in creating or preventing conflict.

1. Divide the class into pairs and distribute Saying It Another Way activity sheets to each pair and have the pairs work together to complete the sheet.

2. When all pairs are done, reassemble the class and have students share their solutions. Pairs might act out their dialogue.

Evaluation:

Students should be able to identify examples of poor communication that lead to conflict.

Students should be able to replace poor communication strategies with good ones.

LET'S FIGHT

Jamal and Sonya had agreed to meet at the library at 2:00 on Saturday to work on their class project. It was due in a week. Sonya waited and waited, but Jamal never came. He was watching basketball on television and forgot about their agreement.

Sonya was furious. This wasn't the first time that Jamal hadn't shown up to work on their project. When she realized Jamal wasn't coming, she marched the three blocks to his house. As she walked, she repeated to herself how thoughtless Jamal was and how angry she was. If she wasn't angry before she started, she certainly was by the time she was pounding on his door.

Jamal came to the door. "Stop banging on the door," he said as he opened the door. "Oh, hi, Sonya. My dad is sleeping; he worked the night shift last night."

Sonya pushed past Jamal. "That's right. It's my fault."

"What are you talking about, Sonya? Oh, no. I forgot I was supposed to meet you at the library," said Jamal and slapped himself on the forehead. "What a dummy!"

"That's right. You are a dummy, a real idiot," snapped Sonya.

"I'm sorry. I forgot. The game got really interesting, and I just forgot, " said Jamal with a look of apology on this face.

"That's not good enough. I'm furious."

"The game is almost over. Why don't we watch the end of it and then we can go to the library? The library is open 'til 6:00," offered Jamal.

"I don't want to watch the game. I think you think this project is some kind of game. It's worth half our grade and it's due in a week. We've barely started," snapped Sonya.

"No. No. It is important, and it's really great that you did the otuline for it. But this is the semi-final game," whined Jamal. By now he was trying to see the game over Sonya's shoulder.

Sonya said huffily, "Well, when you're finished watching the game, I'll be in the library. But don't come looking for me." She gave Jamal one last angry look, turned on her heel, and walked out the door, slamming it shut.

LET'S SOLVE THE PROBLEM

Jamal and Sonya had agreed to meet at the library at 2:00 on Saturday to work on their class project. It was due in a week. Sonya waited and waited, but Jamal never came. He was watching basketball on television and forgot about their agreement.

Sonya was furious. This wasn't the first time that Jamal hadn't shown up to work on their project. When she realized Jamal wasn't coming, she thought about marching over to his house and telling him what she thought of him. But she knew that wouldn't get her what she wanted. Instead, she thought about what to say and how to say it so that she could get what she wanted: Jamal to work with her on their class project.

When she saw Jamal on Monday at school, he tried to avoid her. She went up to him and said calmly, "Hi, Jamal. I want to talk to you about Saturday. I was very sorry that you didn't come."

Jamal stammered, "Yeah, I forgot we were supposed to meet in the library. I'm sorry."

"I can see that you are sorry, but it's still important that you know how I feel. I feel like this project is not important to you."

Jamal grunted. "No, it is, but the game got good and the guys came over afterwards and we went out and I forgot."

Sonya started to get angry so she paused for a moment and didn't say anything. She took a deep breath and when she felt cooler, she said, "If you agree to do something with me, I want you to do it. If for some reason you can't, then call me. My time is important, too."

"If I don't?" said Jamal who was getting angry himself.

"That's not the point," Sonya said. "I'm telling you what I want. Can you do that?"

"Yeah, ok. It was dumb of me to forget. I'm sorry. I'll try to do better. Can you meet me after last period and we'll try the library again? I really need a good grade for our project," Jamal said with a smile.

"Sure, let's try it again," laughed Sonya.

SAYING IT ANOTHER WAY

Below are three descriptions of disagreements that could blow up into conflict. With each description is a good way to communicate and a poor way. Choose the better way to say it, and write a brief dialogue based on the description.

1. Mary is trying to explain how she got red nail polish on Keisha's sweater. Mary is embarrassed and trying to explain and apologize. Keisha is angry. Keisha says: "You're not making any sense." or "Could you explain that again? I don't understand."

2. Rod and Greg got into an argument over the best way to solve a problem in some of Greg's computer software. Rod says: "We can't talk about this because you've already made up your mind." or "I know it's your computer. If you do it the way you want, I think the program will crash."

3. Sally and Lee are arranging their class's exhibit for Parents' Night. They have gotten into an argument over how the display should look. Sally says: "That way of arranging it absolutely will not work." or "That's one way to do it, and here is another way."

2.3 RECOGNIZING THE IMPORTANCE OF HOW YOU SAY IT

GUIDING QUESTION 2:   What are some skills that will help me prevent/resolve conflicts?

SUBJECT AREAS: Social Studies, Health, Language Arts

GROUPING: Whole class, pairs, individuals

MATERIALS: Let's Solve the Problem reading
Videocamera and television monitor
with VCR

BLOOM'S TAXONOMY LEVEL: Comprehension, Analysis, Synthesis, Evaluation

PRODUCTS AND OUTCOMES: Role play of appropriate and inappropriate tone of voice, journal entries

TIME FRAME: 1 class period

Procedure:

1. Explain to students that everyone has a communication style, that is, a way of communicating with others, that is more than talking. Communication style certainly includes words, or what you say, but it also includes how you say it or tone of voice, the way a person carries him-/herself—body language— and the way a person listens. A person's communication style can be positive or negative; it can play a part in creating conflicts or in solving them.

2. Ask students what they think *tone of voice* means. Once a definition has been reached, ask volunteers to repeat the following statements in a tone of voice that might be appropriate for each one:

- A mother saying "I love you" to her baby
- A fan cheering on her/his team "Go, team!"
- The President of the United States addressing the nation in a time of crisis: "Fellow citizens, the hurricane that hit the coast today destroyed 10,000 homes."
- A parent asking his/her child to take out the trash the first time "Please take out the trash."
- A parent asking his/her child the fourth time "Please take out the trash"
- Sonya saying to Jamal "If you agree to do something with me, I want you to do it. If for some reason you can't, then call me. My time is important, too."

3. The last example was from the story of Sonya and Jamal. Explain that ,even though the word choice was good and followed the guidelines for good communication, if Sonya delivered the message in an angry tone of voice, the message would not work. Ask students to explain why.

4. Through a class discussion, lead students to understand that tone of voice needs to match word choice. If the message is serious, the tone of voice should be serious, as when the President is speaking to the nation about an emergency. If the message is light and fun, like a friend asking a friend to go to a game, the tone should match that too. What should the tone be in trying to resolve a disagreement? If one person screams at the other, what will most likely happen? (The other person will lose his/her temper and yell back or disengage from the argument.)

5. Divide the class into pairs and have them act out the following scenario. When students have completed the first role play, they should swap parts and play it out from the beginning again.

   Then ask for several volunteer pairs to act the parts for the whole class. Use the video camera to record the performances for use in Activity 2.4.

Scenario: Two friends were supposed to meet in the public library to work on a class project together. One friend got detention for talking in math class and is half an hour late. The other has to go to work at 4:00 and is angry. The second friend starts to yell at the first. What happens? Continue the conversation.

Assignment: Explain that you know that it is not always easy to focus on the solution to a conflict and tell someone in words rather than show the person through tone of voice how angry you are. Have students reflect in their journals about the following question: When I have a problem or conflict with someone, what would help me focus on calmly telling that person I'm angry and resolving the conflict rather than screaming it and continuing the conflict?

Evaluation:
Students should be able to match appropriate tone of voice to message.

2.4 UNDERSTANDING HOW BODY LANGUAGE CAN CONTRIBUTE TO CONFLICT

Guiding Question 2:   What are some skills that will help me prevent/resolve conflicts?

SUBJECT AREAS: Social Studies, Health, Language Arts

GROUPING: Whole class, small groups

MATERIALS: Videotape of the role plays on word choice from 2.3
Video monitor and VCR

BLOOM'S TAXONOMY LEVEL: Knowledge, Comprehension, Analysis, Evaluation

PRODUCTS AND OUTCOMES: Completed list of body language actions and cues, practice in positive body language, journal entries

TIME FRAME: 1 class period

Procedure:

1. Ask students what they think the term *body language* means. (nonverbal communication) How a person stands, sits, uses his/her hands and arms, and the expression on one's face are all part of communication style and are usually subconscious. Ask students what they think the following actions mean:

   • smiling

   • crossing one's arms

   • looking down while speaking

   • slouching

   The obvious answers are friendliness, anger, embarrassment, disrespect or lack of interest. Other answers could be nervousness, shyness, respect (in some cultures it is disrespectful to look at a parent or someone of authority while speaking to him/her), embarrassment. If you have students from different cultures in your class, spend some time discussing differences in body language and what they mean in each culture. Explain that the context of the situation is important. As tone of voice needs to match the message, so does body language.

2. If you were able to videotape the previous role plays on tone of voice, use that tape now. Play some of the tape of the angry exchanges and ask students to identify the body language that the participants are using. (Finger pointing and staring are probably two that were used.)

If you were unable to videotape the activity, ask two of the more lively participants from the previous activity to replay their roles as best they can remember and ask students to identify the body language.

3. Divide the class into small groups and have each group list different kinds of body language that communicate feelings. Have the groups list different actions and what each says to them. Then have them rate each action as a negative or a positive cue. *Possible responses:* Yawning, nodding head "yes" as someone speaks, shaking head "no" as someone speaks, smiling broadly, pointing at someone, crossing one's arms, frowning, shaking one's fist, holding hands tightly at one's side while speaking, holding one's hands open while speaking, occasionally putting hands on hips, sitting up straight

4. After about 7 minutes, reconvene the class and have a recorder draw a T-table on the board. One side should be labeled Positive and the other side, Negative. Have each group's recorder read aloud its list and indicate whether the action is positive or negative.

5. When all the groups have finished, ask students if they agree with all the ratings. Can circumstances change the meaning of some body language? Have students discuss when and how such changes can occur. Bring in cultural differences.

6. If time permits, have students in pairs act out the different body language cues to get the feel of them. They can practice speaking with both positive and negative actions to see how much looser and more relaxed the positive actions feel.

Assignment: Ask students to describe in their journals how their body language might have contributed to conflict in a recent situation with a friend, parent, or teacher. Students should concentrate on their own actions, not on those of the other person. Student may disguise the situations if they wish.

Evaluation:
Students should be able to describe and explain the difference between positive body language and negative body language and to determine how body language can contribute to conflict.

2.5 DETERMINING LISTENING SKILLS

Guiding Question 2: What are some skills that will help me prevent/resolve conflicts?

SUBJECT AREAS: Social Studies, Health, Language Arts, the Arts

GROUPING: Whole class, pairs

MATERIALS: Videocamera and televison with VCR

I Hear What You Are Saying activity sheets, 1 per student

BLOOM'S TAXONOMY LEVEL: Comprehension, Analysis, Synthesis, Application

PRODUCTS AND OUTCOMES: Completed list of active listening skills, scroll showing active listening skills, active listening skits

TIME FRAME: 1-2 class periods

Procedure:

Pre-class preparation: If possible, prepare the video camera to record the active listening activity in Step 4 below. A tape will allow you to go back over the activity to demonstrate the different techniques during later discussion. You may also wish to record the skits described in Step 6 for discussion.

Also, to demonstrate to students how stories can be altered in the retelling and how rumors begin, write a short incident on a flip chart or on the board before students arrive. Give the story 3 or 4 incidents or lines of dialogue and then cover it so students can't see it.

1. Ask for 6 or 7 volunteers to step into the corridor. Then, uncover the story on the board or flip chart and read it aloud to the class.

2. Ask the first volunteer to come back into the room and tell her/him the story. Be sure the student can't see the flip chart or board but that the rest of the class can. Then, call the second volunteer back into the class and have the first volunteer tell the story to that student. Repeat the activity until the final student tells the story to the class.

3. Now, have students list any differences between the original and final versions of the story. Discuss what this activity shows about how people listen to others. Ask what the activity shows about rumors. What suggestions do students have that might improve the ways they hear and pass on information?

4. Tell them that one process for improving listening skills is called *active listening*. Say that you're going to demonstrate the process for them. Ask them to observe you and take notes on what they think the elements of active listening are. Then, have a volunteer tell you the story from the opening activity. As he/she does, display the various elements of active listening listed below.

- *Get into a listening mode, or frame of mind, and keep an open mind.* Say to yourself aloud before the speaker begins: "I am going to listen. I won't interrupt to try to get my point across. I will wait until he/she is finished. I will respect what he/she has to say."
- *Don't interrupt to state your own ideas.*
- *Use positive body language.* Maintain eye contact. Nod your head or smile.
- *Encourage the speaker to tell you more.* Use statements such as "I'd like to hear more" and "That's really interesting."
- *Restate the speaker's words and feelings.* Use phrases beginning with "You are feeling . . ." or "You think that . . ." or "Do you mean . . ." to ensure that you understand the speaker and keep your mind on his/her words
- *Summarize the other person's points.* This is one last check on the accuracy of your interpretation.
- *Try to find a common point on which you and the speaker agree and say so.*

5. After your demonstration, ask students to list any actions you did that aided in active listening. Have a recorder write the actions on a board master list. Add any they may have missed from the list above. Review the master list, asking students how each item on it aided in active listening. How might active listening reduce conflicts?

6. Divide the class into pairs to practice active listening skills. Distribute the I Hear What You Are Saying activity sheets and ask students to choose one of the situations to create a skit that demonstrates active listening skills. Point out that both parties to the conversation need to demonstrate active listening.

After about 7 minutes, call on volunteers to act out their skits. Have the class identify the active listening skills that each pair demonstrates.

Assignment: Have students create scrolls to display their lists of active listening skills. Display them around the room not only for the duration of the unit but as a reminder throughout the year.

Evaluation:
Students should be able to demonstrate active listening skills and to explain how active listening can contribute to good communication and reduce conflicts.

I HEAR WHAT YOU ARE SAYING

Practice being an active listener by developing a skit with your partner based on one of the suggestions below. Before you begin, study your list of active listening skills. Also remember the following:

- It takes two to have a conversation; each person needs to be a good listener.
- Be sincere and honest; active listening only works if you mean it and if you want it to work.

1. You want to try out for the team but you aren't sure you can make it. You are pretty good at the sport but you don't think you're good enough. You decide to tell your friend about your worries.

   "I want to try out but . . ."

2. Your friend has just gotten an after school job and is excited about it. He/she wants to tell you about it.

   "You know I told you I was applying for a job at . . . ."

3. You've got a problem at home. No one there seems to want to listen to your side of the story. You decide to tell a friend about the situation.

   "I've got to talk to someone about this. . . ."

What Do You Think About Active Listening?

When you've finished preparing your skit, answer the questions below.

1. The hardest thing about active listening is:

   _____

   _____

   _____

   _____

2. The easiest thing about active listening is:

   _____

   _____

   _____

2.6 LEARNING WAYS TO "CALM DOWN"

Guiding Question 2:   What are some skills that will help me prevent/resolve conflicts?

SUBJECT AREAS: Social Studies, Health, the Arts

GROUPING: Individual, whole class, small group

MATERIALS: A variety of art supplies—oaktag paper, crayons, paints, scissors, old magazines for collage illustrations, etc.

BLOOM'S TAXONOMY LEVEL: Knowledge, Comprehension, Analysis, Application, Synthesis

PRODUCTS AND OUTCOMES: Completed list of constructive ways to control one's temper/emotions group displays of calming ideas

TIME FRAME: 1 or 2 class periods

Procedure:

Period 1

1. Without explaining the purpose of the activity, direct students in the following relaxation exercise. Have them wrinkle their foreheads, close their eyes tightly, and clench their teeth. Have them hold this position for five seconds. Then tell them to unwrinkle their foreheads, open their eyes, let their jaws relax and drop open, take a deep breath, and then exhale slowly and and completely. Have them try the same activity, but clenching or tensing their hands, arms, and legs. Tell them that they should concentrate very hard on each step of the activity.

2. When you think a suitable amount of time has elapsed, ask students how the activity makes them feel. Would they say that they are more tense or calmer after the activity?

3. Tell students that what they have just done is one form of relaxation exercise. It is something many people do to calm down when they feel angry or upset. Ask students to think about and suggest other ways of calming down when they are angry or upset. Some examples might be counting to ten, taking a walk, doing some physical activity, taking a deep breath. Have them write these ideas on a sheet of paper.

4. Divide the class into small groups and have the members share their lists. Students should add to their individual lists any good ideas they hear. If some students have only destructive ideas, such as hitting the

wall, point out that such actions only make the problem worse by making the person angrier; such actions feed the anger. Remind students of the boiling point activity in lesson 2.1.

5. Move quickly around the room collecting ideas for calming down from each group. Write the ideas on the board.

6. Have students discuss and analyze the ideas from the master list. They should talk about when and how each of the calming techniques might be used.

Period 2

1. Have students rejoin the groups they were in during the previous period. Direct each group to choose the 10 ideas for calming down that they think are most effective from the master list.

2. Make art materials available to students and tell them that they should create an effective display of their top 10 ideas. They might make illustrated booklets, posters, mobiles, etc.

3. When students have finished, have each group display and answer questions about its presentation.

Alternative: If you wish to confine this activity to one class period or to one period and a small part of another, have individual students select their 10 favorite ways of calming down from the master list. Then have the students, either in class or as an overnight assignment, make fans with their "cool down" tips written on them.

Evaluation:

Students should be able to identify techniques of controlling their emotions constructively when upset and to illustrate those techniques in some way.

MASTER ACTIVITY PLAN

GUIDING QUESTION 3: How can negotiating lead to win-win solutions?

Activities/Description	Math	Science	Language Arts	Social Studies	Health	The Arts	Time
3.1 Taking a Stand for One's Opinion—determining one's point of view on an issue by participating in a continuum exercise, listening to others' opinions			✔	✔	✔		1 class period
3.2 Learning Negotiating Techniques for Win-Win Solutions—determining the value of negotiating strategies			✔	✔	✔		2 class periods
3.3 Practicing Negotiating Techniques—brainstorming solutions to an impasse, creating a poem			✔	✔	✔		1 class period
3.4 Putting Negotiating Strategies to Work—practicing negotiating strategies, analyzing and evaluating negotiating strategies			✔	✔	✔		2-3 class periods

*Page 41 describes a Final Evaluation Activity to check on how well students have recognized and understood techniques they can use to resolve conflicts.

3.1 TAKING A STAND FOR ONE'S OPINION

GUIDING QUESTION 3:   How can negotiating lead to win-win solutions?

SUBJECT AREAS: Social Studies, Health, Language Arts

GROUPING: Whole class, individuals

MATERIALS: Poster board for five signs

BLOOM'S TAXONOMY LEVEL: Comprehension, Analysis, Evaluation

PRODUCTS AND OUTCOMES: Stated student opinions on an issue, journal entries

TIME FRAME: 1 class period

Procedure:

Pre-class preparation: Make five signs large enough for students to hold up and read across the classroom with these labels: Absolutely Agree, Agree Somewhat, Neutral, Disagree Somewhat, Absolutely Disagree. You may wish to consider moving your class to the gym or some other space that has a long, unobstructed wall or corridor in order to do this activity.

1. To help students understand that there will always be conflicts but that people can come to agreements in which everyone can get some of his/her concerns satisfied, select some current issue of interest to your students. It may be a school policy, a community situation, or a national or international event. Formulate a basic statement about that issue.

2. Explain that people can have a variety of opinions about an issue such as the one you have chosen. Some people may agree with it totally. Others may disagree totally. Still others may have a range of opinions between those two opposed points. Such a range of opinions is called a *continuum*. Tell the class that they are going to make a human continuum to show the range of opinions on an issue.

3. Choose two students to represent the two ends of the continuum of opinion. Have them stand at different ends of the longest wall in the room. Give one the sign Absolutely Agree and the other, the sign Absolutely Disagree. Have a third student stand midway between the first two. Explain that this student's position represents balance or neutrality—when there are no strong feelings one way or the other. Give this student the Neutral sign. Finally, have two students stand in positions midway between the center student and those on the two ends. Explain that these students represent positions that agree somewhat, but not totally, with those on the ends. Give one of these students the sign Agree Somewhat and the other, the sign Disagree Somewhat.

4. Now make the statement about the current issue that you formulated earlier. Ask students to think about the statement for a little while and then to take positions that represent their feelings on the continuum formed by the students with the signs. To minimize confusion, ask students to choose their places along the continuum a row at a time.

After everyone has a place, begin asking students why they chose the positions they did. Students may change their positions after each student is finished explaining the reasons for her/his opinions, but students who change positions must explain what prompted the change of opinion.

5. Continue the activity until all students have been heard or until the class begins to lose interest in the exercise. Have everyone return to his/her seat and think about the activity for several minutes. Ask why hearing someone else's point of view may have changed their own opinion. Did someone else's ideas help to clarify their own thinking? Did it point out any inaccurate or incomplete thinking they may have had on the idea?

6. Wrap up the activity by pointing out that, as they learned in Activity 1.1, differences in how people perceive or see something are what conflicts are all about. Ask them to think about and suggest what "lose-lose," "win-lose," and "win-win" solutions might mean.

Assignment: Ask students to write a journal entry in which they think about how hearing and respecting another's point of view can help to prevent conflict.

Evaluation:
Students should be able to articulate a point of view on a topic.

Students should be able to understand how hearing and respecting another's point of view can reduce or eliminate conflict.

3.2 LEARNING NEGOTIATING TECHNIQUES FOR WIN-WIN SOLUTIONS

GUIDING QUESTION 3: How can negotiating lead to win-win solutions?

SUBJECT AREAS: Social Studies, Health, Language Arts

GROUPING: Whole class, small groups

MATERIALS: Win-Win Strategies activity sheets, 1 per small group
Overhead or opaque projector

BLOOM'S TAXONOMY LEVEL: Knowledge, Comprehension, Analysis, Synthesis, Application

PRODUCTS AND OUTCOMES: Completed Win-Win Strategies sheets, journal entries

TIME FRAME: 2 class periods

Procedure:

Period 1

1. Read the following example to students, making up names for the characters: X and Y argue constantly about what TV program to watch, switching the channel back and forth until a parent turns the set off for the evening. Thus, both X and Y lose; it's a lose-lose situation.

   Ask students what lose-lose means, based on this example. Ask how this might become a win-lose situation. (The parent sides with X and lets him/her choose which program to watch.)

2. Divide the class into small groups and ask them to brainstorm a win-win solution, one in which X and Y both get something, although it may not involve watching television. This latter is an important option for the students to hear.

3. Reconvene the class and list the groups' solutions on the board. Discuss whether each is really an example of win-win. Give particular attention to solutions that involve creative answers such as substituting some item for television viewing.

4. Explain that working out win-win solutions requires negotiating. Ask what negotiating is. (a process of reaching an agreement among two or more conflicting points of view) Divide the class into small groups again and give each a Win-Win Strategies sheet. Have the groups answer the questions on the sheets.

5. Record each group's answers on an overhead transparency of the activity sheet or use an opaque projector. Use this as the basis for a class discussion about why negotiating win-win solutions is hard work.

Assignment: Have students write journal entries about how one technique they have learned so far in this unit might help them in negotiating win-win solutions.

Period 2

1. Point out that the Win-Win Strategies that students learned the day before are really ways to prepare for negotiating. Remind students that one of the first steps in negotiating a solution to a problem is clarifying what the disagreement is about. Read the following situation to students and tell them to think what the real issues in the dispute are.

   "Mom, I didn't tell you because I knew you'd say 'no,' but I got a job at Burger Heaven. I start tomorrow. I work Mondays, Tuesdays, and Fridays after school and all day Saturday. I'm making $4.75 an hour."

   "No. You don't need to work."

   "I knew you'd say that. I do need to work. I want to have my own money."

   "You get an allowance and that's all you need. You need to get into college and you can't work and get good grades, too. No."

   "But I can manage my time and . . . ."

   "No, and that's the end of it."

2. Ask students for each person's position and write it on the board. Discuss what each person may be thinking/feeling at this point. What are their reasons, stated and possibly unstated?

3. Divide the class into small groups and have each group brainstorm possible win-win solutions to the situation.

4. Reconvene the class and lead a discussion of the possible solutions, having students answer these questions for the student and for the parent: What do I want? Why do I want it? Which of the solutions do I like? What can I find in common between what I like and what the other person likes? What is most important to me among the reasons? What is most important to the other person? Working with these suggestions, how might I and the other person both get what we want?

   After answering these questions, have the class choose the solution it thinks is best. If there is some dissent, point out that the final strategy is to ask a mediator, or neutral person for his/her opinion.

5. Have students turn the questions in Step 4 into rules or guidelines for choosing the best solution to a problem. They can work in pairs or individually.

Evaluation:

Students should be able to determine the value of win-win solutions.

Students should be able to analyzeand use win-win strategies.

WIN-WIN STRATEGIES

Under each of the strategies, explain its importance in negotiating win-win solutions to disagreements.

Having the Right Attitude

- Be aware of what you are feeling and thinking.

- Know what you really want.

- Know the reasons behind what you want.

- Get your emotions under control.

Getting and Giving the Information

- Set ground rules for the discussion.

- Listen to what the other person is saying.

- Think about what the other person is feeling and thinking.

- State your own reasons clearly and then state your position.

Negotiating the Solution

- Have an open mind.

- Be creative in finding a solution.

3.3 PRACTICING NEGOTIATING TECHNIQUES

GUIDING QUESTION 3: How can negotiating lead to win-win solutions?

SUBJECT AREAS: Social Studies, Health, Language Arts

GROUPING: Whole class, pairs

MATERIALS: *The Sneetches and Other Stories* by Dr. Seuss, Random House, 1961

BLOOM'S TAXONOMY LEVEL: Knowledge, Comprehension, Analysis, Synthesis, Application

PRODUCTS AND OUTCOMES: Poems describing a solution to the Sneetch impasse, class Zax solution booklet

TIME FRAME: 1 class period

Procedure:

1. Read aloud the story "The Zax" by Dr. Seuss. Students should immediately see the problem with being stubborn, rigid, and unwilling to see someone else's point of view.

2. Divide the class into small groups. Half the groups write out the rules of the South-Going Zax and the other half, the rules for the North-Going Zax.

3. Then pair students so that there is one North-Going Zax and one South-Going Zax in each pair. Have each pair brainstorm possible win-win solutions to the Zax's impasse. Give them about 5 minutes to brainstorm, then ask the pairs to choose one solution. Have students spend several minutes working out this solution more fully.

4. After about 5 minutes, have volunteers talk out or act out their solutions for the class. The atmosphere should be one of fun, but students should be using the win-win strategies studied in Activity 3.2.

5. After students have explored the various alternative solutions, have them, working in pairs, write poems in the style of Dr. Seuss to describe their solution to the Zax impasse. Note that in writing the poems students should be using all their conflict resolution and negotiating skills.

6. Reconvene the class and have the pairs share their poems. You may hold a class discussion or vote to determine which solutions students consider the best.

Assignment: Have several volunteers act as publishers and create a booklet *The Zax: The Best Solutions* to publish the class's poems.

Evaluation:

Students should be able to work together to create a solution and write a poem.

3.4 PUTTING NEGOTIATING STRATEGIES TO WORK

GUIDING QUESTION 3: How can negotiating lead to win-win solutions?

SUBJECT AREAS: Social Studies, Health, Language Arts

GROUPING: Pairs, whole group

MATERIALS: Working Out a Win-Win Solution activity sheets, 1 per student
Win-Win Solutions Observation sheets, 1 per student per skit
Win-Win Solutions Evaluation Forms, 1 per student
Videocamera (optional)

BLOOM'S TAXONOMY LEVEL: Comprehension, Synthesis, Application, Evaluation

PRODUCTS AND OUTCOMES: Skits in which conflicts are resolved through win-win negotiation

TIME FRAME: 2-3 class periods

Procedure:

Period 1

Distribute the Working Out a Win-Win Solution activity sheets to students. Allow them time to read the directions and the situations. Have them choose their own partners and begin working on fleshing out one situation and finding a solution. No skit should last longer than 5 minutes. If possible, have a videocamera available so students can tape their skits for presentation to the class.

Periods 2 and 3

1. Have student pairs present their conflict situations and their resolutions.

2. After each presentation, have the class as a whole critique the performance, indicating when the pair used good techniques and strategies and when they might have done better. Distribute one Win-Win Solutions Observation Sheet per student per skit.

Follow Up: After students have presented their skits to the class, distribute the Win-Win Solutions Evaluation Form for student debriefing, one per student.

Evaluation:

Students should be able to demonstrate win-win negotiating strategies for the resolution of a dispute.

Students should be able to evaluate their own negotiating skills objectively.

WORKING OUT A WIN-WIN SOLUTION

Working with a partner, choose one of the situations described below. Then make up dialogue in order to answer the questions and come up with a solution. Use a separate sheet of paper to write your solution.

> **What do you want?**
>
> **Why do you want it?**
> **What does the other person want?**
>
> **Why does he/she want that result?**
>
> **What are some possible solutions?**
>
> **Which solutions do you like?**
>
> **Why do you like them?**
>
> **What interests can you both find to agree on in the possible solutions?**
>
> **What solution can both of you agree on?**

1. A couple has been dating for about a month. She feels that they always do what he wants to do and never what she wants to do. How can they resolve their conflict?

2. You want to go to the basketball game on Tuesday because it is the semifinal for the regional championship. Your parents have a rule about not going out on a school night. How can you convince them that this once won't affect your grades?

3. A friend promised to help you study for the algebra mid-term tomorrow. You were sick for part of the last two weeks and need some tutoring help. Your friend's social studies teacher announces a surprise test for tomorrow. How can you and your friend work out your time conflict?

4. You come from a culture that has very strict rules about what women can and cannot do. You want to go out with your friends to the movies on Saturday night. Your parents do not think this is proper behavior. What can you do?

5. Your science class has been divided into groups to work on projects for the science fair. Each person in a group has a task to do. One of the members of your group is not doing the work. This will affect the results of the project and the group's grade. What can the group do?

WIN-WIN SOLUTIONS OBSERVATION SHEET

After watching the skit, rate the performance of the participants. Make a check in the box that best describes how each participant displayed negotiating skills.

	PERSON A			PERSON B		
In role playing the skit, did the participants remember:	MOST OF THE TIME	SOME OF THE TIME	LITTLE OF THE TIME	MOST OF THE TIME	SOME OF THE TIME	LITTLE OF THE TIME
to identify the problem so they could focus on the solution?						
not to blame the other person?						
to use *I* rather than *you* to tell how each person felt?						
to use a calm, even tone of voice in telling how each felt?						
not to use absolutes like *never* and *always*?						
not to name call?						
to keep an open mind about what the other was saying?						
to use positive body language?						
On the other side of this sheet or on a separate sheet of paper, give examples of positive language that each person used.						
not to interrupt to state own point of view?						
to encourage the other person to explain more?						
On the other side of this sheet or on a separate sheet of paper, explain how each person did this.						
to restate the other person's words and feelings?						
to summarize the other person's points for accuracy?						
to find a common point the two could agree on?						
to use a calming down technique if the person began to get angry or upset?						

This is a good list to keep to remind yourself how to act when you find yourself disagreeing with someone.

WIN-WIN SOLUTIONS EVALUATION FORM

It was only natural that, as you and your partner worked on your skit, the two of you had some differences of opinion. In working on the skit with your partner, did you use the skills you have been learning in this unit?

	MOST OF THE TIME	SOME OF THE TIME	LITTLE OF THE TIME
I kept an open mind about my partner's ideas.			
If I disagreed with any idea, I practiced active listening to hear what my partner was saying.			
I was sure we both understood what the problem was so we could find a solution for it.			
I did not interrupt.			
I looked at my partner as she/he spoke.			
I smiled and nodded as my partner spoke.			
When I spoke, I tried to speak calmly and in a pleasant tone of voice.			
If something did not go well, I didn't blame my partner.			
I didn't call my partner names.			
I tried to explain how I felt rather than tell my partner that he/she was wrong.			
I remembered to use a calming down strategy if I was getting upset or angry.			
I tried to remember to encourage my partner to explain by saying things like "That's interesting. I'd like to know more."			
I restated my partner's words and feelings to show that I was interested and that I actually was listening.			
I summarized my partner's points to be sure I understood them.			
I found that we did agree on some things and used those to reach a solution to our disagreement.			

FINAL EVALUATION ACTIVITY

SUBJECT AREAS: All

GROUPING: Individuals

MATERIALS: Sample Win-Win Solutions Guidelines

BLOOM'S TAXONOMY LEVEL: Comprehension, Synthesis, Application, Evaluation

PRODUCTS AND OUTCOMES: Completed student checklists, journal entries

TIME FRAME: 1 class period

Procedure:

1. As a final activity for *Hearing All Sides: Resolving Conflict,* have each student create a checklist or guidelines for himself or herself of ways to help prevent conflicts and to resolve differences of opinion in a win-win fashion. Students should consider all they have learned about anger triggers, calming down, word choice, tone of voice, body language, and active listening when write their checklists. The Sample Win-Win Solutions Guidelines sheet is an example of such a checklist; however, student lists need not be as detailed as long as they contain the major points.

2. Review each student's listing for accuracy and thoroughness.

3. After students have written their checklists, have them reflect for a few minutes on the strategies described in them. Ask them to think about what is the hardest technique or strategy for them to practice and why. Then ask them to write a journal entry about this difficult strategy and how they can work on doing it.

Optional Activity:

As a further activity, have students decide how to create a permanent reminder of these ways to prevent and resolve conflict. One student might want to letter the items on a scroll, glue the scroll to wood, and varnish it as a plaque. A mobile could be another format. Or a student might want to make several copies and tape one to the inside of his/her locker, another to the door of his /her room, and a third to the refrigerator door, or carry a copy in his/her class notebook. Encourage any project that will help students to internalize and use the strategies.

Evaluation:

Students should be able to recognize and list strategies for preventing conflicts and resolving those that do occur through win-win negotiating.

SAMPLE WIN-WIN SOLUTIONS GUIDELINES

STRATEGIES TO PREVENT CONFLICTS AND MISUNDERSTANDINGS

- Get into a listening frame of mind so I have an open mind.
- Identify the problem so I can focus on the solution.
- Don't blame the other person.
- Don't use absolutes like *never* and *always*.
- Don't name call.
- Use a calm tone of voice.
- Use positive body language cues such as smiling, maintaining eye contact, nodding in agreement, and speaking with open hand gestures.
- Don't interrupt to state my own views.
- Encourage the other person to tell me more by using such statements as "I'd like to hear more."
- Restate the other person's words and feelings to be sure that I understand the speaker and to show I am listening. (This helps me to keep my mind on what the other person is saying, too.)
- Summarize the other person's points to be sure that I understand what the person said and felt.
- Find some ideas that I agree with the other person about and say so.

STRATEGIES FOR A WIN-WIN SOLUTION

In working out a solution, I should answer these questions for myself:

- Know what result I really want.
- Know why I want it.
- Listen to find out what the other person wants.
- Listen to know why he/she wants that result.
- Think of some possible solutions considering what each of us wants.
- Decide which solutions I like.
- Understand why I like them.
- Look for interests the other person and I can find to agree on in the possible solutions.